Andrew Brodie Basics

LET'S DO MULTIPLICATION AND DIVISION

FOR AGES 8–9

with over **100** reward stickers

- Over 400 practice questions
- Regular progress tests
- Matched to the National Curriculum

Published 2016 by Bloomsbury Publishing Plc
50 Bedford Square, London, WC1B 3DP

www.bloomsbury.com

Bloomsbury is a registered trademark of Bloomsbury Publishing Plc

ISBN 978-14729-2634-0

Copyright © 2016 Bloomsbury Publishing
Text copyright © 2016 Andrew Brodie
Cover and inside illustrations of Maurice the Mouse and Andrew Brodie
© 2016 Nikalas Catlow. Other inside illustrations © 2016 Cathy Hughes

A CIP catalogue for this book is available from the British Library.

10 9 8 7 6 5 4 3 2 1

Printed in China by Leo Paper Products

This book is produced using paper that is made from wood grown in managed, sustainable forests. It is natural, renewable and recyclable. The logging and manufacturing processes conform to the environmental regulations of the country of origin.

To see our full range of titles visit **www.bloomsbury.com**

BLOOMSBURY

Introduction

This is the fourth in the series of *Andrew Brodie Basics: Let's Do Multiplication and Division* books. Each book contains more than 400 maths questions, deliberately designed to cover the following key aspects of the 'Number' section of the National Curriculum:

- Number and place value
- Multiplication and division.

Your child will get the most out of this series if you make time to discuss number knowledge as well as basic multiplication and division questions with them. Talk about real life situations, such as how many eggs there would be in sixteen boxes of six. Does your child recognise that the question can be split into a) finding the number of eggs in ten boxes and b) finding the number in six boxes, then adding together the two answers? Mathematically, this can be shown as 16 x 6 = 10 x 6 + 6 x 6. This is known as the Distributive Law.

In Year 4 it is important that children continue to practise the times tables that they have learnt, i.e. the twos, threes, fours, fives, eights and tens, and they extend their knowledge by learning the sixes, sevens, nines, elevens and twelves.

The level of difficulty is increased gradually throughout the book but note that some questions are repeated. For example, the multiplication tables, together with the related division facts, will appear lots of times. This is to ensure that children have the opportunity to learn vital new facts: they may not know the answer to a particular question the first time they encounter it, but this provides the opportunity for you to help them to learn it for the next time that they come across it. Don't be surprised if they need to practise certain questions many times.

You may find that your child is challenged by some questions. Make sure that they don't lose confidence. Instead, encourage them to learn from their mistakes.

In Year 4, children extend their skills by using the facts they already know to solve related questions. For example, because they know that 4 x 2 = 8, they can work out that 4 x 20 = 80 or 40 x 2 = 80, and they can extend this even further by working out that 4 x 200 = 800 or 400 x 2 = 800 or 40 x 20 = 800. Similarly, 8 ÷ 4 = 2 so 80 ÷ 4 = 20, 80 ÷ 2 = 40, 800 ÷ 4 = 200, 800 ÷ 40 = 20 and 800 ÷ 400 = 2. They also continue to learn the processes of short multiplication and short division, extending the work to include multiplying 3-digit numbers by a 1-digit number. These processes are clearly demonstrated and practised in this book.

Children gain confidence by learning facts that they can use in their work. With lots of practice they will see their score improve and will learn to find maths both satisfying and enjoyable.

Look out for...

Maurice the Mouse, who provides useful tips and helpful advice throughout.

Brodie's Fast Five, quick-fire questions designed to test your child's mental arithmetic.

Multiplying by two, five or ten

1 **Time yourself. How quickly can you write out your two times, five times and ten times tables? The first fact for each table has been written for you.**

1 x 2 = 2	1 x 5 = 5	1 x 10 = 10

Look at this fact: $7 \times 5 = 35$

We can use this to find other facts:

$$7 \times 5 = 35$$

$$70 \times 5 = 350 \text{ and } 7 \times 50 = 350 \text{ and } 700 \times 5 = 3500$$
$$\text{and } 7 \times 500 = 3500 \text{ and } 70 \times 50 = 3500$$

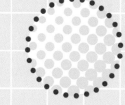

Now try these.

2 3 x 5 =

3 30 x 5 =

4 300 x 5 =

5 6 x 2 =

6 60 x 2 =

7 600 x 2 =

8 4 x 10 =

9 40 x 10 =

Multiplying by two, five or ten

Do you remember how you can use the multiplication tables to find divisions?

Remember, because 6 x 2 = 12, then 12 ÷ 2 = 6 and 12 ÷ 6 = 2.

1   18 ÷ 2 =

2   24 ÷ 2 =

3   6 ÷ 2 =

4   12 ÷ 2 =

5   16 ÷ 2 =

6   22 ÷ 2 =

7   10 ÷ 2 =

8   14 ÷ 2 =

Remember, because 7 x 5 = 35, then 35 ÷ 7 = 5 and 35 ÷ 5 = 7.

9   30 ÷ 5 =

10   55 ÷ 5 =

11   15 ÷ 5 =

12   60 ÷ 5 =

13   25 ÷ 5 =

14   45 ÷ 5 =

15   10 ÷ 5 =

16   35 ÷ 5 =

Remember, because 6 x 10 = 60, then 60 ÷ 6 = 10 and 60 ÷ 10 = 6.

17   60 ÷ 10 =

18   120 ÷ 10 =

19   40 ÷ 10 =

20   70 ÷ 10 =

21   20 ÷ 10 =

22   80 ÷ 10 =

23   110 ÷ 10 =

24   90 ÷ 10 =

Brodie's Fast Five

7 x 5 =

6 x 5 =

9 x 5 =

12 x 5 =

15 x 5 =

These questions are easy if you know the two times table.

Look at this question:

$$34 \times 2$$

There are three tens.

There are four units.

We are multiplying by two units.

To multiply 34 and 2 we can write them one above the other. We say that the 4 and the 2 are in the units column. The 3 is in the tens column.

```
  3  4          3  4          3  4
x    2        x    2        x    2
_____      _____      _____
                 6  8          6  8
```

We multiply the 4 by the 2 units first, which is 8. We write the 8 underneath.

Next, we multiply the 3 tens by the 2 units. The final answer is 68.

Sometimes when we multiply there are enough units to make an extra ten.

```
  3  7          3  7          3  7
x    2        x    2        x    2
_____      _____      _____
                    4          7  4
                 1             1
```

7 units x 2 units is enough to make a ten and 4 units, because 7 x 2 = 14. We write the 1 ten under the tens column, ready to add it on.

Next, we multiply the 3 tens by the 2 units to make 6 tens, and we add on the extra 1 ten to give a total of 7 tens. The final answer is 74.

Use short multiplication to answer the questions on this page.

The first question has been done for you.

1   **23 x 2 =**

```
      2   3
  x       2
  _____
      4   6
```

5   **38 x 2 =**

2   **12 x 2 =**

6   **46 x 2 =**

3   **32 x 2 =**

7   **28 x 2 =**

4   **43 x 2 =**

8   **36 x 2 =**

Brodie's Fast Five

6 x 5 =   **9 x 5 =**

7 x 10 =   **12 x 5 =**   **8 x 5 =**

Use short multiplication to answer the questions on this page.

The first question has been done for you.

1   **13 x 5 =**

```
      1   3
  x       5
  _____
      6   5
      1
```

5   **19 x 5 =**

2   **15 x 5 =**

6   **12 x 5 =**

3   **17 x 5 =**

7   **16 x 5 =**

4   **14 x 5 =**

8   **18 x 5 =**

Brodie's Fast Five

6 x 2 =   **9 x 10 =**

7 x 10 =   **12 x 2 =**   **9 x 5 =**

1 Write out the two, five and ten times tables as fast as you can.

| 1 x 2 = 2 | 1 x 5 = 5 | 1 x 10 = 10 |
| 2 x 2 = 4 | 2 x 5 = 10 | 2 x 10 = 20 |

2 How many sets of two make eighteen altogether?

3 How many fives make twenty?

4 How many tens make one hundred?

5 How many twos make twenty-four?

6 How many fives make forty-five?

7 How many tens make a hundred and twenty?

Use short multiplication to answer these questions.

8 27 x 2 =

10 36 x 2 =

9 15 x 5 =

11 18 x 5 =

Multiplying by two, four or eight

The two, four and eight times tables are closely related.

1 Time yourself. How quickly can you write out your two times, four times and eight times tables? The first fact for each table has been written for you.

1 x 2 = 2	1 x 4 = 4	1 x 8 = 8

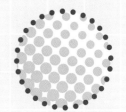

Look at this fact: $6 \times 4 = 24$

We can use this to find other facts:

$$6 \times 4 = 24$$

$60 \times 4 = 240$ and $6 \times 40 = 240$ and $600 \times 4 = 2400$
and $6 \times 400 = 2400$ and $60 \times 40 = 2400$

Now try these.

2 $7 \times 8 =$

3 $70 \times 8 =$

4 $700 \times 8 =$

5 $4 \times 4 =$

6 $40 \times 4 =$

7 $400 \times 4 =$

8 $3 \times 8 =$

9 $30 \times 80 =$

Dividing by two, four or eight

The multiplication tables help with divisions.

Remember, because 8 x 2 = 16, then 16 ÷ 2 = 8 and 16 ÷ 8 = 2.

1   18 ÷ 2 =

2   24 ÷ 2 =

3   10 ÷ 2 =

4   6 ÷ 2 =

5   12 ÷ 2 =

6   22 ÷ 2 =

7   16 ÷ 2 =

8   14 ÷ 2 =

Remember, because 7 x 4 = 28, then 28 ÷ 4 = 7 and 28 ÷ 7 = 4.

9   20 ÷ 4 =

10   44 ÷ 4 =

11   56 ÷ 4 =

12   72 ÷ 4 =

13   36 ÷ 4 =

14   84 ÷ 4 =

15   16 ÷ 4 =

16   48 ÷ 4 =

Remember, because 6 x 8 = 48, then 48 ÷ 6 = 8 and 48 ÷ 8 = 6.

17   16 ÷ 8 =

18   96 ÷ 8 =

19   56 ÷ 8 =

20   32 ÷ 8 =

21   48 ÷ 8 =

22   24 ÷ 8 =

23   64 ÷ 8 =

24   88 ÷ 8 =

Brodie's Fast Five

7 x 4 =   12 x 4 =

6 x 8 =   5 x 8 =   9 x 8 =

Multiplying by eight can make some big numbers.

Look at this example:

73 x 8

There are seven tens.　**There are three units.**　**We are multiplying by eight units.**

```
    7  3              7  3                7  3
x      8          x      8            x      8
_____         _____           _____
                         4            5  8  4
                      2                  2
```

We multiply the 3 units by the 8 units first, which gives 24. We write the 4 in the units column and carry the 2 tens over. We write the 2 under the tens column.

Now we multiply the 7 tens by the 8 units to give 56. Add the 2 tens that were carried over, so we have 58 tens, which are enough for 5 hundreds and 8 tens.

Now try these. The first one has been done for you.

1　**34 x 8**

```
    3  4
x      8
_____
2  7  2
   3
```

3　**84 x 8**

2　**49 x 8**

4　**76 x 8**

Use short multiplication to answer the questions on this page.

The first one has been done for you.

1 46 x 4

```
      4   6
  x       4
  ─────────
  1   8   4
      2
```

5 38 x 4

2 73 x 8

6 68 x 8

3 59 x 4

7 37 x 4

4 99 x 8

8 37 x 8

Brodie's Fast Five

8 x 8 = ☐   4 x 8 = ☐

12 x 8 = ☐   9 x 8 = ☐   6 x 8 = ☐

Short multiplication problems

I wouldn't want to wrestle an octopus!

Use short multiplication to answer the questions on this page.

1 There are four wheels on each car. How many wheels are there altogether on forty-seven cars?

3 There are four chairs at each table. How many chairs are needed for sixty-two tables?

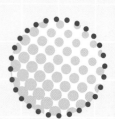

wheels

chairs

2 There are eight pears in each bag. How many pears are there altogether in twenty-five bags?

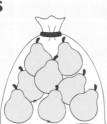

4 Each octopus has eight arms. How many arms do thirty-six octopuses have altogether?

pears

arms

Brodie's Fast Five

7 x 8 =   12 x 10 =

9 x 4 =   3 x 8 =   14 x 2 =

1 Write out the two, four and eight times tables as fast as you can.

| 1 x 2 = | 1 x 4 = | 1 x 8 = |
| 2 x 2 = | 2 x 4 = | 2 x 8 = |

2 How many fours make twenty-eight?

3 How many eights make forty?

4 How many fours make forty-eight?

5 How many eights make thirty-two?

6 How many fours make thirty-six?

7 How many eights make seventy-two?

Use short multiplication to answer these questions.

8 An octopus has eight arms. How many arms do thirty-nine octopuses have altogether?

9 A car has four wheels. How many wheels do ninety-nine cars have altogether?

arms

wheels

Multiplying by three, six or nine

You need to know the facts for the three, six and nine times tables.

Look closely at the three, six and nine times tables below.

1 x 3 = 3	1 x 6 = 6	1 x 9 = 9
2 x 3 = 6	2 x 6 = 12	2 x 9 = 18
3 x 3 = 9	3 x 6 = 18	3 x 9 = 27
4 x 3 = 12	4 x 6 = 24	4 x 9 = 36
5 x 3 = 15	5 x 6 = 30	5 x 9 = 45
6 x 3 = 18	6 x 6 = 36	6 x 9 = 54
7 x 3 = 21	7 x 6 = 42	7 x 9 = 63
8 x 3 = 24	8 x 6 = 48	8 x 9 = 72
9 x 3 = 27	9 x 6 = 54	9 x 9 = 81
10 x 3 = 30	10 x 6 = 60	10 x 9 = 90
11 x 3 = 33	11 x 6 = 66	11 x 9 = 99
12 x 3 = 36	12 x 6 = 72	12 x 9 = 108

Look at this fact: **8 x 6 = 48**

We can use this to find other facts:

8 x 6 = 48

80 x 6 = 480 and **8 x 60 = 480** and **800 x 6 = 4800**
and **8 x 600 = 4800** and **80 x 60 = 4800**

Now try these.

1   7 x 6 =

2   70 x 6 =

3   700 x 6 =

4   4 x 9 =

5   40 x 9 =

6   400 x 9 =

7   8 x 3 =

8   80 x 30 =

The multiplication tables help with divisions.

Remember, because 8 x 3 = 24, then 24 ÷ 3 = 8 and 24 ÷ 8 = 3.

1   18 ÷ 3 =

2   24 ÷ 3 =

3   36 ÷ 3 =

4   3 ÷ 3 =

5   9 ÷ 3 =

6   12 ÷ 3 =

7   21 ÷ 3 =

8   15 ÷ 3 =

Remember, because 7 x 6 = 42, then 42 ÷ 6 = 7 and 42 ÷ 7 = 6.

9   18 ÷ 6 =

10   42 ÷ 6 =

11   72 ÷ 6 =

12   30 ÷ 6 =

13   48 ÷ 6 =

14   54 ÷ 6 =

15   60 ÷ 6 =

16   12 ÷ 6 =

Remember, because 6 x 9 = 54, then 54 ÷ 9 = 6 and 54 ÷ 6 = 9.

17   99 ÷ 9 =

18   27 ÷ 9 =

19   54 ÷ 9 =

20   18 ÷ 9 =

21   45 ÷ 9 =

22   9 ÷ 9 =

23   63 ÷ 9 =

24   81 ÷ 9 =

Brodie's Fast Five

7 x 9 =

12 x 9 =

4 x 9 =

8 x 9 =

10 x 9 =

Use short multiplication to answer the questions on this page.

The first one has been done for you.

1 | 46 x 3

	4	6
x		3
1	3	8
	1	

5 | 47 x 6

2 | 58 x 6

6 | 72 x 9

3 | 29 x 9

7 | 85 x 3

4 | 76 x 3

8 | 77 x 6

Brodie's Fast Five

6 x 9 =

7 x 6 =

9 x 8 =

4 x 9 =

8 x 6 =

Short multiplication problems

Use short multiplication to answer the questions on this page.

1 There are three wheels on each tricycle. How many wheels are there altogether on twenty-three tricycles?

wheels

3 There are nine players in a baseball team. How many players are there altogether in nineteen teams?

players

2 There are six eggs in each box. How many eggs are there altogether in eighteen boxes?

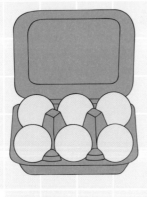

eggs

4 Each octopus has eight arms. How many arms do forty-two octopuses have?

arms

Brodie's Fast Five

8 x 9 =   11 x 9 =

12 x 6 =   7 x 6 =   13 x 3 =

Practising the six times table

Do you know the six times table?

1 **Write out the six times table as fast as you can.**

$1 \times 6 =$ ⬜

$2 \times 6 =$ ⬜

⬜ ⬜

⬜ ⬜

⬜ ⬜

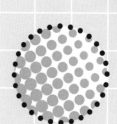

There are six eggs in a box.

2 How many eggs are needed to fill eight boxes? ⬜

3 How many boxes could be filled if there are twenty-four eggs? ⬜

4 How many eggs are needed to fill twelve boxes? ⬜

5 How many boxes could be filled if there are thirty-six eggs? ⬜

6 How many eggs are needed to fill five boxes? ⬜

7 How many boxes could be filled if there are seventy-two eggs? ⬜

8 How many eggs are needed to fill nine boxes? ⬜

9 How many boxes could be filled if there are fifty-four eggs? ⬜

Brodie's Fast Five

$3 \times 6 =$ ⬜ $6 \times 6 =$ ⬜

$6 \times 5 =$ ⬜ $12 \times 6 =$ ⬜ $6 \times 9 =$ ⬜

1 **Write out the three, six and nine times tables**

1 x 3 =	1 x 6 =	1 x 9 =
2 x 3 =	2 x 6 =	2 x 9 =

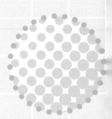

2 36 ÷ 6 =

3 27 ÷ 3 =

4 54 ÷ 9 =

5 81 ÷ 9 =

6 48 ÷ 6 =

7 9 ÷ 3 =

8 63 ÷ 9 =

9 72 ÷ 6 =

10 36 ÷ 3 =

Use short multiplication to answer these questions.

11 There are three wheels on a tricycle. How many wheels are there altogether on nineteen tricycles?

12 There are six eggs in a box. How many eggs are there altogether in twenty-five boxes?

wheels

eggs

Multiplying by seven, eleven or twelve

You need to know the facts for the seven, eleven and twelve times tables.

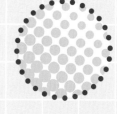

Look carefully at the seven, eleven and twelve times tables below.

1 x 7 = 7	1 x 11 = 11	1 x 12 = 12
2 x 7 = 14	2 x 11 = 22	2 x 12 = 24
3 x 7 = 21	3 x 11 = 33	3 x 12 = 36
4 x 7 = 28	4 x 11 = 44	4 x 12 = 48
5 x 7 = 35	5 x 11 = 55	5 x 12 = 60
6 x 7 = 42	6 x 11 = 66	6 x 12 = 72
7 x 7 = 49	7 x 11 = 77	7 x 12 = 84
8 x 7 = 56	8 x 11 = 88	8 x 12 = 96
9 x 7 = 63	9 x 11 = 99	9 x 12 = 108
10 x 7 = 70	10 x 11 = 110	10 x 12 = 120
11 x 7 = 77	11 x 11 = 121	11 x 12 = 132
12 x 7 = 84	12 x 11 = 132	12 x 12 = 144

Look at this fact: 6 x 7 = 42

We can use this to find other facts:

6 x 7 = 42

60 x 7 = 420 **and** 6 x 70 = 420 **and** 600 x 7 = 4200 **and** 6 x 700 = 4200 **and** 60 x 70 = 4200

Now try these.

 1   8 x 7 =

2   80 x 7 =

3   800 x 7 =

4   80 x 70 =

5   10 x 7 =

6   100 x 7 =

7   10 x 70 =

8   10 x 700 =

The multiplication tables help with divisions.

Remember, because 4 x 7 = 28, then 28 ÷ 4 = 7 and 28 ÷ 7 = 4.

1   35 ÷ 7   = ☐   **5**   49 ÷ 7   = ☐

2   84 ÷ 7   = ☐   **6**   21 ÷ 7   = ☐

3   42 ÷ 7   = ☐   **7**   77 ÷ 7   = ☐

4   14 ÷ 7   = ☐   **8**   28 ÷ 7   = ☐

Remember, because 7 x 11 = 77, then 77 ÷ 11 = 7 and 77 ÷ 7 = 11.

9   88 ÷ 11 = ☐   **13**   121 ÷ 11 = ☐

10   22 ÷ 11 = ☐   **14**   55 ÷ 11 = ☐

11   77 ÷ 11 = ☐   **15**   132 ÷ 11 = ☐

12   99 ÷ 11 = ☐   **16**   44 ÷ 11 = ☐

Remember, because 6 x 12 = 72, then 72 ÷ 12 = 6 and 72 ÷ 6 = 12.

17   96 ÷ 12 = ☐   **21**   36 ÷ 12 = ☐

18   24 ÷ 12 = ☐   **22**   12 ÷ 12 = ☐

19   48 ÷ 12 = ☐   **23**   60 ÷ 12 = ☐

20   84 ÷ 12 = ☐   **24**   132 ÷ 12 = ☐

Brodie's Fast Five

6 x 7 = ☐   12 x 7 = ☐

8 x 7 = ☐   3 x 7 = ☐   9 x 7 = ☐

Short multiplication by seven

Use short multiplication to answer the questions on this page.

The first question has been done for you.

1 38 x 7

```
      3   8
  x       7
  ─────────
  2   6   6
      5
```

2 69 x 7

3 28 x 7

4 46 x 7

5 97 x 7

6 82 x 7

7 75 x 7

8 54 x 7

Brodie's Fast Five

9 x 12 =   12 x 12 =

4 x 12 =   7 x 12 =   8 x 12 =

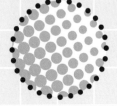
What is your favourite day of the week?

Use short multiplication to answer the questions on this page.

1 There are seven days in a week. How many days are there altogether in seventeen weeks?

4 How many days are there altogether in twenty-five weeks?

2 How many days are there altogether in thirty-two weeks?

5 How many days are there altogether in twenty-nine weeks?

3 How many days are there altogether in forty-seven weeks?

6 How many days are there altogether in fifty-two weeks?

Brodie's Fast Five

6 x 11 =

9 x 11 =

10 x 11 =

12 x 11 =

11 x 11 =

Practising the seven times table

1 Write out the seven times table as fast as you can.

1 x 7 =

2 x 7 =

2 How many days are there in eight weeks?

6 How many days are there in twenty weeks?

3 If my birthday is in forty-nine days' time, how many weeks do I have to wait?

7 If my sister's birthday is in sixty-three days' time, how many weeks does she have to wait?

4 How many days are there in twelve weeks?

8 How many days are there in thirteen weeks?

5 I'm going to a show in eighty-four days' time. How many weeks do I have to wait?

9 My brother is going to a football match in forty-two days' time. How many weeks does he have to wait?

1 Write out the seven, eleven and twelve times tables.

1 x 7 =	1 x 11 =	1 x 12 =
2 x 7 =	2 x 11 =	2 x 12 =

2 35 ÷ 7 =

3 24 ÷ 12 =

4 77 ÷ 11 =

5 84 ÷ 7 =

6 48 ÷ 12 =

7 132 ÷ 12 =

8 70 ÷ 7 =

9 121 ÷ 11 =

10 96 ÷ 12 =

Use short multiplication to answer these questions.

11 There are seven days in a week. How many days are there altogether in twenty-four weeks?

12 How many days are there altogether in sixteen weeks?

days

days

Now that you're so good at multiplying two numbers together, let's try doing the same with three!

Look at this question: $5 \times 2 \times 3$

To find the answer to the question, you need to do two multiplication sums. You can choose which order to do these in:

You can do 5×2 **then multiply the answer by** 3:

$5 \times 2 = 10$ **then** $10 \times 3 = 30$

or

You can do 2×3 **then multiply by** 5:

$2 \times 3 = 6$ **then** $6 \times 5 = 30$

or

You can do 5×3 **then multiply by** 2:

$5 \times 3 = 15$ **then** $15 \times 2 = 30$

Did you notice that all three answers were the same?

Now try these.

1 $3 \times 4 \times 5 =$

4 $5 \times 10 \times 2 =$

2 $2 \times 4 \times 3 =$

5 $10 \times 4 \times 2 =$

3 $2 \times 10 \times 3 =$

6 $3 \times 6 \times 10 =$

Multiplying three numbers together part 2

Look at this question: **7 x 6 x 3**

To answer the question, you need to do two multiplication sums. You can choose which order to do these in:

You can do **7 x 6** then multiply by **3**:

$7 \times 6 = 42$

	4	2
x		3
1	2	6

You can do **6 x 3** then multiply by **7**:

$6 \times 3 = 18$

	1	8
x		7
1	2	6
	5	

You can do **7 x 3** then multiply by **6**:

$7 \times 3 = 21$

	2	1
x		6
1	2	6

Now try these. Remember, you can do the multiplications in any order.

1 8 x 4 x 6 =

3 7 x 8 x 3 =

2 9 x 4 x 7 =

4 6 x 9 x 4 =

Lots of eggs

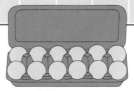

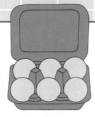

1 Here is a box of six eggs. How many of these boxes are needed for seventy-two eggs?

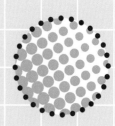

3 Here is a box of twelve eggs. How many of these boxes are needed for seventy-two eggs?

2 Here is a box of nine eggs. How many of these boxes are needed for seventy-two eggs?

Look at these boxes of eggs.

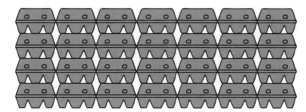

4 There are six eggs in each box. How many eggs are there altogether?

The question on this page is called a correspondence problem.

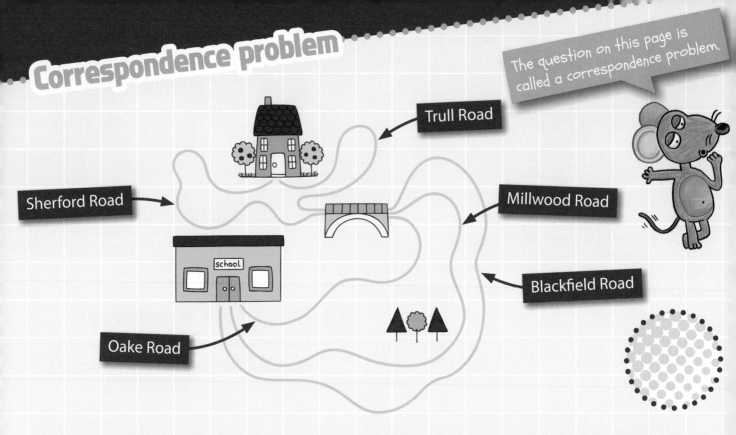

Abi can walk to school from her house. She can choose from two different roads to get to the bridge. Once she has crossed the bridge, she can choose from three different roads to get to school. Write down all the possible combinations of routes that Abi could choose. The first one has been done for you.

1 Sherford Road   **then**   Oake Road

2   **then**

3   **then**

4   **then**

5   **then**

6   **then**

Brodie's Fast Five

6 x 12 =   12 x 12 =

9 x 12 =   11 x 12 =   7 x 12 =

Do you know the eight times table?

1   **Write out the eight times table as fast as you can.**

$1 \times 8 =$

$2 \times 8 =$

A spider has eight legs.

2   **How many legs are there on seven spiders?**

3   **How many legs are there on seventeen spiders?**

4   **How many legs are there on twenty-seven spiders?**

5   **How many legs are there on thirty-seven spiders?**

There are eight iced buns in a pack.

6   **How many iced buns are needed to fill ten packs?**

7   **How many packs can be filled if there are ninety-six iced buns?**

8   **How many packs can be filled if there are seventy-two iced buns?**

9   **How many packs can be filled if there are fifty-six iced buns?**

1 2 x 4 x 5 =

2 5 x 4 x 3 =

3 2 x 6 x 3 =

4 5 x 2 x 2 =

5 2 x 2 x 2 =

6 3 x 3 x 3 =

Use short multiplication to answer these questions.

7 9 x 9 x 9

9 7 x 7 x 7

8 8 x 8 x 8

10 6 x 6 x 6

Short division explanation page

Look at this question:

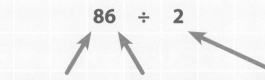

$$86 \div 2$$

There are eight tens.   There are six units.   We are dividing by two units.

To divide 86 by 2 we can write the question out like this:

```
        4              4  3
2 | 8  6        2 | 8  6        2 | 8  6
```

We divide the 8 by the 2 first, which is 4. We then write the 4 above the 8.

Then we divide the 6 by the 2, which is 3. We then write the 3 above the 6. The final answer is 43.

Sometimes when we divide the tens, there is one or more spare ten, which can be broken into extra units.

```
              2              2  7
3 | 8  1     3 | 8  ²1     3 | 8  ²1
```

3 goes into 8 two times, so we write the 2 above the 8. However, there are 2 tens left over that we carry over to the units column, so that there are 21 units.

Now divide the 21 units by 3, which gives 7 units. The final answer is 27.

Short division

Use short division to answer the questions on this page. The first one has been done for you.

You can look back at page 33 if you need help.

1 26 ÷ 2

$$\begin{array}{c|cc} & 1 & 3 \\ \hline 2 & 2 & 6 \end{array}$$

5 58 ÷ 2

2 84 ÷ 2

6 76 ÷ 2

3 46 ÷ 2

7 98 ÷ 2

4 80 ÷ 2

8 72 ÷ 2

Brodie's Fast Five

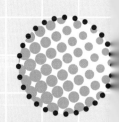

28 ÷ 7 =   48 ÷ 6 =

96 ÷ 8 =   72 ÷ 12 =   56 ÷ 7 =

More short division

Are you feeling confident with short division?

Use short division to answer the questions on this page. The first one has been done for you.

1 39 ÷ 3

$$3 \overline{)\,3\;9\,}$$
      1 3

2 72 ÷ 4

3 85 ÷ 5

4 90 ÷ 6

5 90 ÷ 2

6 90 ÷ 3

7 91 ÷ 7

8 78 ÷ 6

Brodie's Fast Five

63 ÷ 7 =   54 ÷ 6 =

72 ÷ 8 =   108 ÷ 12 =   36 ÷ 6 =

35

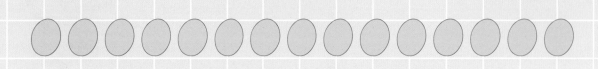

Divisions with remainders

A remainder is what is 'left over'.

Sometimes divisions have remainders. Look at this example:

There are fifteen eggs. The eggs need to be sorted into boxes, with six in each box.

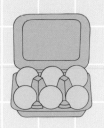 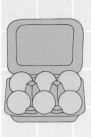

There are enough eggs for two boxes of six, and there are three eggs left over.

We can write the mathematical sentence like this: $15 \div 6 = 2\ r3$

This letter 'r' means 'remainder'. The remainder shows what is left over.

Now try these.

1	$56 \div 6 =$		5	$47 \div 6 =$
2	$28 \div 6 =$		6	$32 \div 6 =$
3	$39 \div 6 =$		7	$26 \div 6 =$
4	$19 \div 6 =$		8	$64 \div 6 =$

Brodie's Fast Five

$11 \div 2 =$ ___ $19 \div 2 =$ ___

$17 \div 2 =$ ___ $23 \div 2 =$ ___ $15 \div 2 =$ ___

Be careful! Not all of the divisions on this page have remainders.

There are 15 eggs.

Or, the eggs could be sorted into 3 sets of 5 with no remainder.

$15 \div 5 = 3$

The eggs could be sorted into 5 sets of 3 with no remainder.

$15 \div 3 = 5$

If we sorted the eggs into sets of 2, there would be 7 sets with 1 spare egg.

$15 \div 2 = 7 \text{ r}1$

Look at some of the other ways that we could sort the eggs:

Into sets of 4: $15 \div 4 = 3 \text{ r}3$
Into sets of 6: $15 \div 6 = 2 \text{ r}3$
Into sets of 8: $15 \div 8 = 1 \text{ r}7$
Into sets of 9: $15 \div 9 = 1 \text{ r}6$

Now try sorting 18 eggs into the following sets. Write the division sentence for each question. The first one has been done for you.

1 In sets of 2: $18 \div 2 = 9$ 5 In sets of 6:

2 In sets of 3:   6 In sets of 7:

3 In sets of 4:   7 In sets of 8:

4 In sets of 5:   8 In sets of 9:

Brodie's Fast Five

13 x 2 =   13 x 3 =

13 x 4 =   13 x 5 =   13 x 6 =

Use short division to answer these questions.

1 88 ÷ 2

5 85 ÷ 5

2 84 ÷ 6

6 92 ÷ 4

3 87 ÷ 3

7 96 ÷ 6

4 76 ÷ 4

8 98 ÷ 7

The questions below have remainders.

9 47 ÷ 5 =

11 68 ÷ 7 =

10 44 ÷ 6 =

12 68 ÷ 8 =

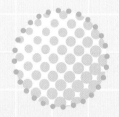

Practising the nine times table

1 Write out the nine times table as fast as you can.

$1 \times 9 =$

$2 \times 9 =$

There are nine cupcakes in a pack.

2 How many cupcakes are there in seven packs?

3 How many cupcakes are there in thirteen packs?

4 How many cupcakes are there in twenty-three packs?

5 How many cupcakes are there in forty-eight packs?

6 How many cupcakes are needed to fill twelve packs?

7 How many packs can be filled if there are eighty-one cupcakes?

8 How many packs can be filled if there are ninety-nine cupcakes?

9 How many packs can be filled if there are a hundred and eighty cupcakes?

It's easy to multiply three-digit numbers by one-digit numbers.

Look at this question:

247   x   8

There are two hundreds.   **There are four tens.**   **There are seven units.**   **We are multiplying by eight units.**

	2	4	7
x			8
			6
		5	

	2	4	7
x			8
1	9	7	6
	3	5	

	2	4	7
x			8
1	9	7	6
	3	5	

We multiply the 7 units by the 8 units first, which is 56, so we write the 6 in the units column and carry the 5 to underneath the tens column.

Next, we multiply the 4 tens by the 8 units to get 32. We then add the 5 tens we carried over, to make 37. We write the 7 in the tens column, and we carry the 3 to underneath the hundreds column.

Now we multiply the 2 by the 8 to give 16. We add the 3 that we carried over, so that we now have enough for 9 hundreds and 1 thousand. The final answer is 1976.

Now try these.

 1   346 x 8

 3   732 x 8

 2   419 x 8

 4   654 x 8

Do you know the twelve times table?

1 **Write out the twelve times table as fast as you can.**

1 x 12 =		
2 x 12 =		

There are twelve months in a year.

2 **How many months are there in seven years?**

3 **How many months are there in twelve years?**

4 **How many months are there in nine years?**

5 **How many months are there in twenty years?**

6 **How many years can be made from twenty-four months?**

7 **How many years can be made from forty-eight months?**

8 **How many years can be made from ninety-six months?**

9 **How many years can be made from seventy-two months?**

More short multiplication of three-digit numbers

Remember, you can look back at page 40 if you need help.

Use short multiplication to answer the questions on this page. The first one has been done for you.

1 476 x 3

```
      4   7   6
  x           3
  1   4   2   8
      2   1
```

5 347 x 6

2 958 x 6

6 712 x 5

3 729 x 9

7 885 x 2

4 786 x 7

8 777 x 4

Brodie's Fast Five

13 x 9 =   13 x 8 =

13 x 6 =   13 x 4 =   13 x 7 =

More short division

I bet you're quick at short division!

Use short division to answer the questions on this page. The first question has been done for you.

1 57 ÷ 3

$$
\begin{array}{r}
1\ \ 9 \\
3\overline{\smash{\big)}\,5\,{}^2 7}
\end{array}
$$

5 70 ÷ 2 =

2 84 ÷ 4 =

6 87 ÷ 3 =

3 95 ÷ 5 =

7 98 ÷ 7 =

4 84 ÷ 6 =

8 75 ÷ 5 =

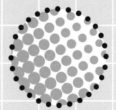

Brodie's Fast Five

91 ÷ 7 =   78 ÷ 6 =

104 ÷ 8 =   156 ÷ 12 =   65 ÷ 5 =

Use short multiplication to answer the questions.

| 1 | 682 x 3 | | 4 | 243 x 7 |

| 2 | 499 x 7 | | 5 | 519 x 9 |

| 3 | 867 x 8 | | 6 | 742 x 6 |

Use short division to answer the questions.

| 7 | 80 ÷ 5 | | 10 | 86 ÷ 2 |

| 8 | 90 ÷ 6 | | 11 | 84 ÷ 3 |

| 9 | 69 ÷ 3 | | 12 | 92 ÷ 4 |

ANSWERS

Page 3 • Multiplying by two, five or ten

1.

1 x 2 = 2	1 x 5 = 5	1 x 10 = 10
2 x 2 = 4	2 x 5 = 10	2 x 10 = 20
3 x 2 = 6	3 x 5 = 15	3 x 10 = 30
4 x 2 = 8	4 x 5 = 20	4 x 10 = 40
5 x 2 = 10	5 x 5 = 25	5 x 10 = 50
6 x 2 = 12	6 x 5 = 30	6 x 10 = 60
7 x 2 = 14	7 x 5 = 35	7 x 10 = 70
8 x 2 = 16	8 x 5 = 40	8 x 10 = 80
9 x 2 = 18	9 x 5 = 45	9 x 10 = 90
10 x 2 = 20	10 x 5 = 50	10 x 10 = 100
11 x 2 = 22	11 x 5 = 55	11 x 10 = 110
12 x 2 = 24	12 x 5 = 60	12 x 10 = 120

2. 15
3. 150
4. 1500
5. 12
6. 120
7. 1200
8. 40
9. 400

Page 4 • Dividing by two, five or ten

1. 9
2. 12
3. 3
4. 6
5. 8
6. 11
7. 5
8. 7

9. 6
10. 11
11. 3
12. 12
13. 5
14. 9
15. 2
16. 7

17. 6
18. 12
19. 4
20. 7
21. 2
22. 8
23. 11
24. 9

Brodie's Fast Five

1. 35
2. 45
3. 30
4. 60
5. 75

Page 6 • Short multiplication by two

1. 46
2. 24
3. 64
4. 86
5. 76
6. 92
7. 56
8. 72

Brodie's Fast Five

1. 30
2. 45
3. 70
4. 60
5. 40

Page 7 • Short multiplication by five

1. 65
2. 75
3. 85
4. 70
5. 95
6. 60
7. 80
8. 90

Brodie's Fast Five

1. 12
2. 90
3. 70
4. 24
5. 45

Page 8 • Progress Test 1

1.

1 x 2 = 2	1 x 5 = 5	1 x 10 = 10
2 x 2 = 4	2 x 5 = 10	2 x 10 = 20
3 x 2 = 6	3 x 5 = 15	3 x 10 = 30
4 x 2 = 8	4 x 5 = 20	4 x 10 = 40
5 x 2 = 10	5 x 5 = 25	5 x 10 = 50
6 x 2 = 12	6 x 5 = 30	6 x 10 = 60
7 x 2 = 14	7 x 5 = 35	7 x 10 = 70
8 x 2 = 16	8 x 5 = 40	8 x 10 = 80
9 x 2 = 18	9 x 5 = 45	9 x 10 = 90
10 x 2 = 20	10 x 5 = 50	10 x 10 = 100
11 x 2 = 22	11 x 5 = 55	11 x 10 = 110
12 x 2 = 24	12 x 5 = 60	12 x 10 = 120

2. 9
3. 4
4. 10
5. 12
6. 9
7. 12

8. 54
9. 30
10. 72
11. 90

Page 9 • Multiplying by two, four or eight

1.

1 x 2 = 2	1 x 4 = 4	1 x 8 = 8
2 x 2 = 4	2 x 4 = 8	2 x 8 = 16
3 x 2 = 6	3 x 4 = 12	3 x 8 = 24
4 x 2 = 8	4 x 4 = 16	4 x 8 = 32
5 x 2 = 10	5 x 4 = 20	5 x 8 = 40
6 x 2 = 12	6 x 4 = 24	6 x 8 = 48
7 x 2 = 14	7 x 4 = 28	7 x 8 = 56
8 x 2 = 16	8 x 4 = 32	8 x 8 = 64
9 x 2 = 18	9 x 4 = 36	9 x 8 = 72
10 x 2 = 20	10 x 4 = 40	10 x 8 = 80
11 x 2 = 22	11 x 4 = 44	11 x 8 = 88
12 x 2 = 24	12 x 4 = 48	12 x 8 = 96

2. 56
3. 560
4. 5600
5. 16
6. 160
7. 1600
8. 24
9. 2400

Page 10 • Dividing by two, four or eight

1. 9
2. 12
3. 5
4. 3
5. 6
6. 11
7. 8
8. 7

9. 5
10. 11
11. 14
12. 18
13. 9
14. 21
15. 4
16. 12

17. 2
18. 12
19. 7
20. 4
21. 6
22. 3
23. 8
24. 11

Brodie's Fast Five

1. 28
2. 48
3. 48
4. 40
5. 72

Page 11 • Short multiplication explanation page

1. 272
2. 392
3. 672
4. 608

Page 12 • Short multiplication by four or eight

1. 184
2. 584
3. 236
4. 792
5. 152
6. 544
7. 148
8. 296

Brodie's Fast Five

1. 64
2. 32
3. 96
4. 72
5. 48

Page 13 • Short multiplication problems

1. 188
2. 200
3. 248
4. 288

Brodie's Fast Five

1. 56
2. 120
3. 36
4. 24
5. 28

Page 14 • Progress Test 2

1.

1 x 2 = 2	1 x 4 = 4	1 x 8 = 8
2 x 2 = 4	2 x 4 = 8	2 x 8 = 16
3 x 2 = 6	3 x 4 = 12	3 x 8 = 24
4 x 2 = 8	4 x 4 = 16	4 x 8 = 32
5 x 2 = 10	5 x 4 = 20	5 x 8 = 40
6 x 2 = 12	6 x 4 = 24	6 x 8 = 48
7 x 2 = 14	7 x 4 = 28	7 x 8 = 56
8 x 2 = 16	8 x 4 = 32	8 x 8 = 64
9 x 2 = 18	9 x 4 = 36	9 x 8 = 72
10 x 2 = 20	10 x 4 = 40	10 x 8 = 80
11 x 2 = 22	11 x 4 = 44	11 x 8 = 88
12 x 2 = 24	12 x 4 = 48	12 x 8 = 96

2. 7
3. 5
4. 12
5. 4
6. 9
7. 9

8. 312
9. 396

Page 15 • Multiplying by three, six or nine

1. 42
2. 420
3. 4200
4. 36
5. 360
6. 3600
7. 24
8. 2400

Page 16 • Dividing by three, six or nine

1. 6
2. 8
3. 12
4. 1
5. 3
6. 4
7. 7
8. 5

9. 3
10. 7
11. 12
12. 5
13. 8
14. 9
15. 10
16. 2

17. 11
18. 3
19. 6
20. 2
21. 5
22. 1
23. 7
24. 9

Brodie's Fast Five

1. 63
2. 108
3. 36
4. 72
5. 90

Page 17 • Short multiplication by three, six or nine

1. 138
2. 348
3. 261
4. 228
5. 282
6. 648
7. 255
8. 462

Brodie's Fast Five

1. 54
2. 72
3. 42
4. 36
5. 48

Page 18 • Short multiplication problems

1. 69
2. 108
3. 171
4. 336

Brodie's Fast Five

1. 72
2. 99
3. 72
4. 42
5. 39

Page 19 • Practising the six times table

1.

$1 \times 6 = 6$
$2 \times 6 = 12$
$3 \times 6 = 18$
$4 \times 6 = 24$
$5 \times 6 = 30$
$6 \times 6 = 36$
$7 \times 6 = 42$
$8 \times 6 = 48$
$9 \times 6 = 54$
$10 \times 6 = 60$
$11 \times 6 = 66$
$12 \times 6 = 72$

2. 48
3. 4
4. 72
5. 6
6. 30
7. 12
8. 54
9. 9

Brodie's Fast Five

1. 18
2. 36
3. 30
4. 72
5. 54

Page 20 • Progress Test 3

1.

$1 \times 3 = 3$	$1 \times 6 = 6$	$1 \times 9 = 9$
$2 \times 3 = 6$	$2 \times 6 = 12$	$2 \times 9 = 18$
$3 \times 3 = 9$	$3 \times 6 = 18$	$3 \times 9 = 27$
$4 \times 3 = 12$	$4 \times 6 = 24$	$4 \times 9 = 36$
$5 \times 3 = 15$	$5 \times 6 = 30$	$5 \times 9 = 45$
$6 \times 3 = 18$	$6 \times 6 = 36$	$6 \times 9 = 54$
$7 \times 3 = 21$	$7 \times 6 = 42$	$7 \times 9 = 63$
$8 \times 3 = 24$	$8 \times 6 = 48$	$8 \times 9 = 72$
$9 \times 3 = 27$	$9 \times 6 = 54$	$9 \times 9 = 81$
$10 \times 3 = 30$	$10 \times 6 = 60$	$10 \times 9 = 90$
$11 \times 3 = 33$	$11 \times 6 = 66$	$11 \times 9 = 99$
$12 \times 3 = 36$	$12 \times 6 = 72$	$12 \times 9 = 108$

2. 6
3. 9
4. 6
5. 9
6. 8
7. 3
8. 7
9. 12
10. 12

11. 57
12. 150

Page 21 • Multiplying by seven, eleven or twelve

1. 56
2. 560
3. 5600
4. 5600
5. 70
6. 700
7. 700
8. 7000

Page 22 • Dividing by seven, eleven or twelve

1. 5
2. 12
3. 6
4. 2
5. 7
6. 3
7. 11
8. 4

9. 8
10. 2
11. 7
12. 9
13. 11
14. 5
15. 12
16. 4

17. 8
18. 2
19. 4
20. 7
21. 3
22. 1
23. 5
24. 11

Brodie's Fast Five

1. 42
2. 84
3. 56
4. 21
5. 63

Page 23 • Short multiplication by seven

1. 266
2. 483
3. 196
4. 322
5. 679
6. 574
7. 525
8. 378

Brodie's Fast Five

1. 108
2. 144
3. 48
4. 84
5. 96

Page 24 • Short multiplication problems

1. 119
2. 224
3. 329
4. 175
5. 203
6. 364

1. 66
2. 99
3. 110
4. 132
5. 121

Page 25 • Practising the seven times table

1.
$1 \times 7 = 7$
$2 \times 7 = 14$
$3 \times 7 = 21$
$4 \times 7 = 28$
$5 \times 7 = 35$
$6 \times 7 = 42$
$7 \times 7 = 49$
$8 \times 7 = 56$
$9 \times 7 = 63$
$10 \times 7 = 70$
$11 \times 7 = 77$
$12 \times 7 = 84$

2. 56
3. 7
4. 84
5. 12
6. 140
7. 9
8. 91
9. 6

Page 26 • Progress Test 4

1 .

$1 \times 7 = 7$	$1 \times 11 = 11$	$1 \times 12 = 12$
$2 \times 7 = 14$	$2 \times 11 = 22$	$2 \times 12 = 24$
$3 \times 7 = 21$	$3 \times 11 = 33$	$3 \times 12 = 36$
$4 \times 7 = 28$	$4 \times 11 = 44$	$4 \times 12 = 48$
$5 \times 7 = 35$	$5 \times 11 = 55$	$5 \times 12 = 60$
$6 \times 7 = 42$	$6 \times 11 = 66$	$6 \times 12 = 72$
$7 \times 7 = 49$	$7 \times 11 = 77$	$7 \times 12 = 84$
$8 \times 7 = 56$	$8 \times 11 = 88$	$8 \times 12 = 96$
$9 \times 7 = 63$	$9 \times 11 = 99$	$9 \times 12 = 108$
$10 \times 7 = 70$	$10 \times 11 = 110$	$10 \times 12 = 120$
$11 \times 7 = 77$	$11 \times 11 = 121$	$11 \times 12 = 132$
$12 \times 7 = 84$	$12 \times 11 = 132$	$12 \times 12 = 144$

2. 5
3. 2
4. 7
5. 12
6. 4
7. 11
8. 10
9. 11
10. 8
11. 168
12. 112

Page 27 • Multiplying three numbers together part 1

1. 60
2. 24
3. 60
4. 100
5. 80
6. 180

Page 28 • Multiplying three numbers together part 2

1. 192
2. 252
3. 168
4. 216

Page 29 • Lots of eggs

1. 12
2. 8
3. 6
4. 168

Page 30 • Correspondence problem

1. Sherford Road then Oake Road
2. Sherford Road then Millwood Road
3. Sherford Road then Blackfield Road
4. Trull Road then Oake Road
5. Trull Road then Millwood Road
6. Trull Road then Blackfield Road

1. 72
2. 144
3. 108
4. 132
5. 84

Page 31 • Practising the eight times table

1.
$1 \times 8 = 8$
$2 \times 8 = 16$
$3 \times 8 = 24$
$4 \times 8 = 32$
$5 \times 8 = 40$
$6 \times 8 = 48$
$7 \times 8 = 56$
$8 \times 8 = 64$
$9 \times 8 = 72$
$10 \times 8 = 80$
$11 \times 8 = 88$
$12 \times 8 = 96$

2. 56
3. 136
4. 216
5. 296
6. 80
7. 12
8. 9
9. 7

Page 32 • Progress Test 5

1. 40
2. 60
3. 36
4. 20
5. 8
6. 27
7. 729
8. 512
9. 343
10. 216

Page 34 • Short division

1. 13
2. 42
3. 23
4. 40
5. 29
6. 38
7. 49
8. 36

1. 4
2. 8
3. 12
4. 6
5. 8

Page 35 • More short division

1. 13
2. 18
3. 17
4. 15
5. 45
6. 30
7. 13
8. 13

1. 9
2. 9
3. 9
4. 9
5. 6

Page 36 • Divisions with remainders

1. 9 r2
2. 4 r4
3. 6 r3
4. 3 r1
5. 7 r5
6. 5 r2
7. 4 r2
8. 10 r4

1. 5 r1 or $5\frac{1}{2}$
2. 9 r1 or $9\frac{1}{2}$
3. 8 r1 or $8\frac{1}{2}$
4. 11 r1 or $11\frac{1}{2}$
5. 7 r1 or $7\frac{1}{2}$

Page 37 • More divisions with remainders

1. $18 \div 2 = 9$
2. $18 \div 3 = 6$
3. $18 \div 4 = 4$ r2
4. $18 \div 5 = 3$ r3
5. $18 \div 6 = 3$
6. $18 \div 7 = 2$ r4
7. $18 \div 8 = 2$ r2
8. $18 \div 9 = 2$

1. 26
2. 39
3. 52
4. 65
5. 78

Page 38 • Progress Test 6

1. 44
2. 14
3. 29
4. 19
5. 17
6. 23
7. 16
8. 14
9. 9 r2
10. 7 r2
11. 9 r5
12. 8 r4

Page 39 • Practising the nine times table

1.
1 x 9 = 9
2 x 9 = 18
3 x 9 = 27
4 x 9 = 36
5 x 9 = 45
6 x 9 = 54
7 x 9 = 63
8 x 9 = 72
9 x 9 = 81
10 x 9 = 90
11 x 9 = 99
12 x 9 = 108

2. 63
3. 117
4. 207
5. 432
6. 108
7. 9
8. 11
9. 20

Page 40 • Short multiplication of three-digit numbers

1. 2768
2. 3352
3. 5856
4. 5232

Page 41 • Practising the twelve times table

1.
1 x 12 = 12
2 x 12 = 24
3 x 12 = 36
4 x 12 = 48
5 x 12 = 60
6 x 12 = 72
7 x 12 = 84
8 x 12 = 96
9 x 12 = 108
10 x 12 = 120
11 x 12 = 132
12 x 12 = 144

2. 84
3. 144
4. 108
5. 240
6. 2
7. 4
8. 8
9. 6

Page 42 • More short multiplication of three-digit numbers

1. 1428
2. 5748
3. 6561
4. 5502
5. 2082
6. 3560
7. 1770
8. 3108

Brodie's Fast Five

1. 117
2. 104
3. 78
4. 52
5. 91

Page 43 • More short division

1. 19
2. 21
3. 19
4. 14
5. 35
6. 29
7. 14
8. 15

Brodie's Fast Five

1. 13
2. 13
3. 13
4. 13
5. 13

Page 44 • Progress Test 7

1. 2046
2. 3493
3. 6936
4. 1701
5. 4671
6. 4452

7. 16
8. 15
9. 23
10. 43
11. 28
12. 23